PERU

A TRUE BOOK

by
Elaine Landau

Children's Press®

A Division of Grolier Publishing

New York London Hong Kong Sydney
Danbury, Connecticut

Peruvian folk dancers

Reading Consultant
Linda Cornwell
*Coordinator of School Quality
and Professional Improvement
Indiana State Teachers
Association*

Author's Dedication
For Joshua Garmizo

Visit Children's Press® on the
Internet at:
http://publishing.grolier.com

Library of Congress Cataloging-in-Publication Data

Peru / by Elaine Landau.
   p.   cm.—(A true book)
Includes bibliographical references and index.
Summary: Discusses the history, geography, people, government, and economy of Peru.
ISBN: 0-516-21174-9 (lib. bdg.)   0-516-27019-2 (pbk.)
1. Peru—Juvenile literature. [1. Peru.] I. Title. II. Series.
F3408.5.L36 2000
985—dc21   99-14955
                                             CIP
                                           AC

Contents

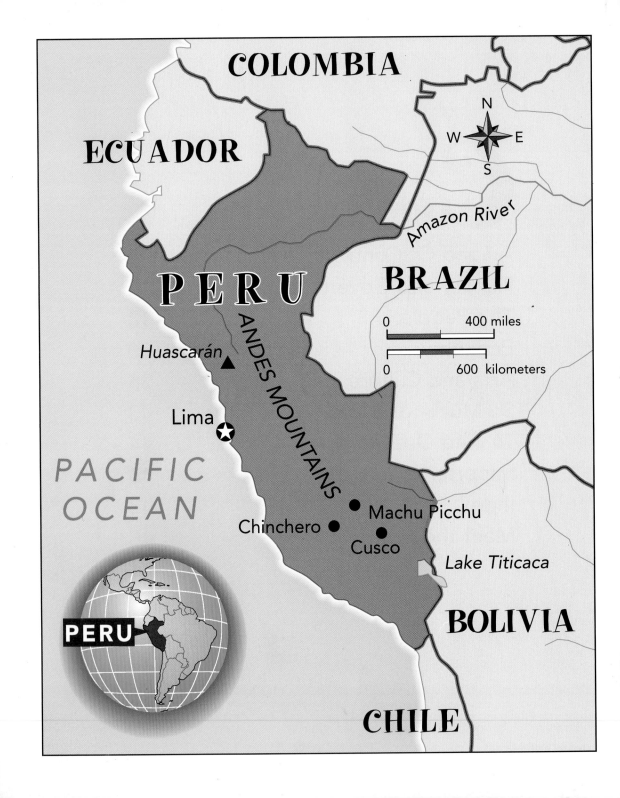

A Land of Contrasts

There's a country in South America that may seem like many countries rolled into one. It has a desert, a coastline, snowcapped mountains, tropical rain forests and bustling cities. It is the third-largest country on the continent (after Brazil and Argentina). It's Peru.

Peru is bordered by Ecuador and Colombia to the north and by Brazil to the east. Bolivia and Chile lie to the south, while the Pacific Ocean is off Peru's west coast. Thanks to its tropical location and unusual land-scape, Peru has a greater variety of plants and wildlife than most places. Peru is also home to the world's largest rodent, the capybara, and the scarlet macaw.

Capybara (right) are swamp animals, while blue yellow and scarlet macaw (below) are found in Peru's rain forests.

Peru has three major geographic regions. They are the coastal region, the Andes Mountains, and the rain forest.

A view of Peru's coast

The coastal region is a long, narrow strip of land along the Pacific Ocean. It is 1,554 miles (2,500 kilometers) long but only 40 to 100 miles (64 to 160 km) wide. Peru's largest cities and farming areas lie in this region. Although much of the land is desert, fifty mountain rivers flow across it. These rivers supply drinking water for the cities as well as water for crops.

The Andes Mountains region runs through Peru from north to south. There you'll find the alpaca, a beautiful species of the camel family that is prized for its fleecy wool. The mountains

A herd of alpacas cross the snowy Andes Mountain terrain.

divide Peru's coast from its rain forest. The Peruvian Andes are the world's second-highest mountains. Only the Himalaya in south Asia are higher. Huascarán, an extinct volcano, is Peru's highest peak at 22,205 feet (6,768 meters). Lake Titicaca is the largest lake in South America and the highest navigable lake in the world.

The tropical rain forest is Peru's largest area, covering more than half its land. But even though most of Peru is rain forest, only a tiny part of the country's popula-

Reed boats on the shores of Lake Titicaca (above); The Amazon River, and the rain forest

tion lives there. Peru's rain forest region contains lush plant growth and a vast network of rivers, including the Amazon River.

History and Government

The first people who lived in Peru probably came from North America. Over the centuries, a number of civilizations developed there. Perhaps the best known was the Inca Empire. By about A.D. 1200, the wealthy Inca Empire stretched as far north as Colombia and Ecuador

Ruins of the ancient Inca civilization (top); An Inca poncho (left) and silver drinking cups (right), probably made for a wealthy person or for use in rituals

and as far south as Chile and Argentina. The Inca built fabulous monuments, palaces, and temples. They made fine cloth and fashioned magnificent jewelry and ornaments of gold and silver.

In 1532, Spanish troops led by explorer Francisco Pizarro

Francisco Pizarro founded Peru's capital, Lima, after he defeated the Inca.

invaded Peru and conquered the Inca. The country was a Spanish colony for the next three hundred years. During that time, life was extremely hard for the Inca. The Spaniards took their freedom as well as their gold. The Inca were forced to convert to Christianity and work long hours in Spanish-owned mines and on plantations. At times they rebelled, but these uprisings were quickly crushed.

Peru declared its independence from Spain in 1821. A few years later, a constitution was written to make the country a democratic republic. Since then, Peru has had many different kinds of government.

In 1992, with the army's support, Peru's president, Alberto Fujimori, made many changes in the country's constitution and its government. He called for new elections

President Alberto Fujimori

and a new constitution. Some people believed in Fujimori, but others accused him of being a dictator. He was supported by many of the poor people in the rural areas. In 1995, Fujimori was reelected president.

The People

Peru's population reflects the country's history. A large portion of the people are mestizos (mes-TEE-zohs). They are from mixed Native American and Spanish families. Almost half of the people are Native Americans. A smaller group are white and

This young girl, a mestiza, lives in the Andes Mountains.

descendants of European families, mostly Spanish. A small number have black African ancestry or are Asian. Peru has two official languages—

Spanish and Quechua, a Native American language. Some of the Native American people in the rain forests speak other languages, as well.

Most people in Peru are Roman Catholics. There are small groups of Protestants,

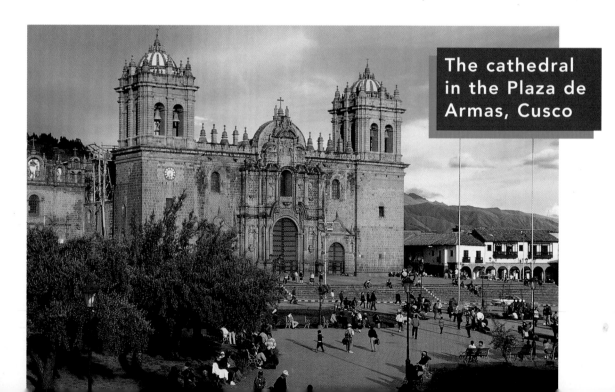

The cathedral in the Plaza de Armas, Cusco

Jews, Muslims, and Buddhists. Freedom of religion exists in Peru today.

There are great differences in the lifestyles of Peruvians. These differences began when the Spanish invaders seized power and the country's riches. The upper class is still mostly white. But over the years, as the Spanish and the Native Americans mingled and married, a middle class of mestizos developed. Many middle-class mestizos have good jobs in

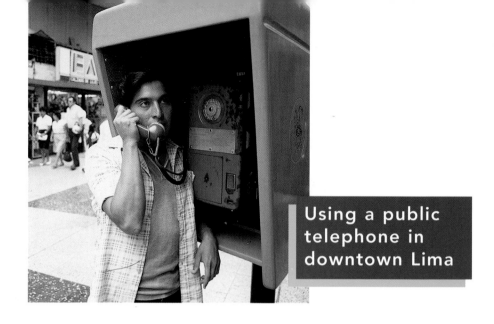

Using a public telephone in downtown Lima

business, government, and the army. Most of the Native Americans are poor people with very little schooling.

Upper- and middle-class Peruvians tend to live in the country's large cities and dress like people in the United States and Europe do.

Some have large homes with enclosed patios. Others live in high-rise apartment buildings.

Most of Peru's Native Americans live in the high Andes Mountains and farm for a living. Some wear Western clothing but many of the older people prefer the traditional handwoven garments of their people. Small tribes of Native Americans still live in Peru's rain forests—hunting, fishing, and gathering roots and fruits. These tribes wear

A Quechua family (left); Yagua Indians (below) in Peruvian rain forests

little clothing due to the hot weather and their way of life.

Some Native Americans live in the cities, but few of them

are middle- or upper-class. It's hard for these people to survive in the cities. Often they lack schooling and speak only their tribal language. Many do not have the job skills needed to get work that pays well.

In Peru, people often eat foods that reflect the area they live in. Mountain people eat mainly potatoes, maize, or corn, and other vegetables. They raise chickens, geese, turkeys, ducks, and even guinea pigs, which are eaten on special

Chickens are washed and seasoned in preparation for a community feast.

occasions. People who live on the coast eat a lot of fresh fish and spicy chicken and rice dishes. In the cities, street vendors sell chunks of grilled beef on bamboo sticks.

Children in Peru are required to attend school from age six to fifteen. But many young people don't go to school at all. The shortage of schools and teachers in rural areas frequently affects Native American children. Upper- and middle-class young people usually attend private schools, and many go on to one of Peru's forty-six universities.

Children in a Lima school review a lesson with their teacher.

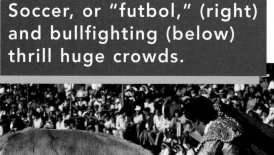

Soccer, or "futbol," (right) and bullfighting (below) thrill huge crowds.

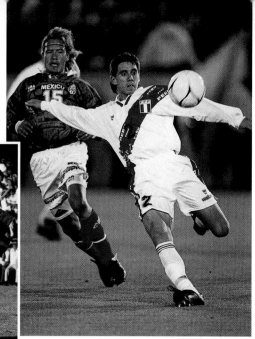

Soccer and bullfighting are popular sports in Peru. The country has several professional Peruvian soccer teams, and large crowds attend the bullfights. Other favorites include basketball, horse racing, and volleyball.

¡Fiesta!

Many Peruvian towns hold fiestas, or festivals, to celebrate religious holidays and agricultural events. People wear traditional, colorful costumes and enjoy music, dancing, and feasting. In February or March, Carnaval is observed. On June 24, an ancient Inca festival features dancing and parades. Peru's Independence Day is celebrated on July 28. People visit family graves on All Souls Day, November 2, and bring gifts of flowers and food.

A masked procession

Flame dancers at Carnaval

Economy

Peru's natural resources make it one of the world's top seven mining countries. Much of the world's copper, gold, and silver is found in Peru, as well as a small amount of zinc. Minerals make up about half of Peru's exports.

A copper processing plant (left) and transport area (below)

The Pacific Ocean is an important resource for the nation's fishing industry. Tons of fish, mainly anchovies, are caught off the country's

Fishermen load the night's catch onto refrigerated trucks.

coast each year, making Peru the world's leading producer of fish meal. High-quality fish, such as sole and Pacific snapper, are also exported.

Farming is an important industry in Peru, and much of the population is involved in it.

Large amounts of potatoes, wheat, cotton, coffee, and sugarcane are grown for export. Other crops, such as beans, corn, and rice, provide food for Peruvians.

In addition, Peru has many factories. They make chemicals,

A sugarcane factory

rubber, steel, paper products, and cars, as well as processed foods and fabrics.

Through the years, Peru has had its share of problems with high unemployment and inflation. However, during the 1990s the government took steps to encourage the growth of business. Poverty is still widespread, but conditions in some areas have improved.

Art and Culture

The art and culture of Peru reflect its special mixture of people. Traditional Native American music is heard throughout the country, as well as popular mestizo bands. The work of Peruvian artists and writers captures

Folk dancers perform the Marinera, a traditional Peruvian dance (left). Mimes provide entertainment in a public square (below).

much of their country's history and natural beauty.

Theater has long been popular in Peru. Plays, ballets, and folk-dance performances are favorites there. The National Institute of Culture encourages Peru's artists and tries to make their work available to the public.

Native American handicrafts from Peru are highly sought after by tourists and collectors, especially handmade silver jewelry and brightly colored textiles. Many visitors come to

A native woman displays her skill at weaving.

Peru today to admire the remains of its ancient civilizations. A splendid example is the ruins of an Inca city at Machu Picchu, high in the Andes.

Annie's Peak

Mount Huascarán

After four tries, at the age of fifty-eight Annie Smith Peck set a world record in 1908 by climbing the highest peak in the Western hemisphere—Mount Huascarán. The government of Peru awarded her a medal, and named the spot after her—Cumbre Ana Peck (Annie's Peak). Annie returned to the United States, where she wrote a book about her adventures. At the age of sixty-one, Annie returned to Peru and climbed to the top of Mount Coropuna.

Annie Smith Peck

So Much to See

Peru offers much for visitors to explore. Cusco, the capital city of the Inca, contains the ruins of great royal palaces and temples as well as attractive plazas. Other interesting sites include Ollantaytambo Village, one of the few places where people still live in houses built by the Inca.

The Inca village of Ollantaytambo (above); market day in the Andes Mountains (left)

At Chinchero (Village of the Rainbow), people still follow many ancient customs from pre-Hispanic times. For example, the villagers still barter, or trade, various farm products at their colorful Sunday market.

Peru also has more government-protected land than any of the surrounding countries. The land is managed by the National Institute of Natural Resources. In recent years, many tourists have come to visit Peru's rain forest. The area has been called "the world's largest pharmacy," or drugstore, because of the huge number of healing plants found there.

Without a doubt, Peru is a land rich in history and natural wonders.

A mountain pool reflects the beauty of Peru.

To Find Out More

Here are some additional resources to help you learn more about the nation of Peru:

Books

Blue, Rose and Corinne Naden. **The Andes Mountains.** Raintree Steck-Vaughn, 1994.

Buell, Janet. **Ice Maiden of the Andes.** Twenty-First Century Books, 1997.

Landau, Elaine. **Mountain Mammals.** Children's Press, 1996.

Parker, Edward. **Ecuador, Peru, Bolivia.** Raintree Steck-Vaughn, 1998.

Pitkanen, Matti A. **The Grandchildren of the Incas.** Carolrhoda Books, 1991.

Rogers, Barbara Radcliffe. **Peru.** Gareth Stevens, 1992.

Organizations and Online Sites

AlpacaNet
http://www.alpacanet.com

Learn about this unusual animal's connection to the ancient civilization of the Inca, and ways its prized fleece is used by fiber artists and weavers. Check out events, such as alpaca fairs and seminars, that may be happening near your town.

Descendants of the Incas
http://www.incas.org

This site shares images and information about the Native American culture of the Andes. Find out about making and dyeing yarn, and click on photos of the community.

Peru Explorer
http://www.peru-explorer.com

A guide to Peruvian culture, sites, and cities, featuring natural attractions and ecotourist adventures.

Includes tips on money, local time, and weather. Check out the animated tree full of parrots!

Rain Forest Action Network: Kids Corner
http://www.ran.org/ran/kids __action/indexl.htm/

Learn about the native people and animals of the rain forest, join the Kids Action Team, and follow eight steps for helping to preserve the rain forests.

South American Explorers Club
U.S. Headquarters
126 Indian Creek Road
Ithaca, New York 14850
http://www.samexplo.org

A non-profit organization making information available about South and Central American people, cultures, geography, and more. A good resource for maps, guidebooks, and travel tips.

Important Words

agricultural related to farming

convert to change one's religion or other beliefs

democratic republic a system in which all people have equal rights

dictator someone who has complete control of a country, often ruling it unjustly

export to send to other countries for sale or trade

fish meal ground dried fish and fish waste, used as fertilizer and animal food

inflation an increase in prices

navigable deep and wide enough for ships to sail across

species a type of plant or animal

unemployment the state of being without a job or work of any kind

Index

Meet the Author

Elaine Landau worked as a newspaper reporter, an editor, and a youth services librarian before becoming a full-time writer. She has written more than one hundred nonfiction books for young people, including True Books on dinosaurs, animals, countries, and food.

Ms. Landau, who has a bachelor's degree in English and journalism from New York University and a master's degree in library and information science from Pratt Institute, lives in Florida with her husband and son.